United States Government Accountability Offic

Report to Congressional Re

September 2014

CLOUD COMPUTING

Additional Opportunities and Savings Need to Be Pursued

GAO Highlights

Highlights of GAO-14-753, a report to congressional requesters

CLOUD COMPUTING

Additional Opportunities and Savings Need to Be Pursued

Why GAO Did This Study

Cloud computing is a relatively new process for acquiring and delivering computing services via information technology (IT) networks. Specifically, it is a means for enabling on-demand access to shared and scalable pools of computing resources with the goal of minimizing management effort and service provider interaction. To encourage federal agencies to pursue the potential efficiencies associated with cloud computing, the Office of Management and Budget (OMB) issued a "Cloud First" policy in 2011 that required agency Chief Information Officers to implement a cloud-based service whenever there was a secure, reliable, and cost-effective option.

GAO was asked to assess agencies' progress in implementing cloud services. GAO's objectives included assessing selected agencies' progress in using such services and determining the extent to which the agencies have experienced cost savings. GAO selected for review the seven agencies that it reported on in 2012 in order to compare their progress since then in implementing cloud services; the agencies were selected using the size of their IT budgets and experience in using cloud services. GAO also analyzed agency cost savings and related documentation and interviewed agency and OMB officials.

What GAO Recommends

GAO is recommending, among other things, that the seven agencies assess the IT investments identified in this report that have yet to be evaluated for suitability for cloud computing services. Of the seven agencies, six agreed with GAO's recommendations, and one had no comments.

View GAO-14-753. For more information, contact David Powner at (202) 512-9286 or pownerd@gao.gov.

What GAO Found

Each of the seven agencies reviewed implemented additional cloud computing services since GAO last reported on their progress in 2012. For example, since then, the total number of cloud computing services implemented by the agencies increased by 80 services, from 21 to 101. The agencies also added to the amount they reported spending on cloud services by $222 million, from $307 million to $529 million. Further, the agencies increased the percentage of their information technology (IT) budgets allocated to cloud services; however, as shown in the table, the overall increase was just 1 percent.

Amount Agencies Allocated to Cloud Services (for Fiscal Years 2012 and 2014)

Department/Agency	Percent of IT budget reported spent on cloud in 2012	Percent budgeted for cloud in 2014
Agriculture	1	3
General Services Administration	2	5
Health and Human Services	0	1
Homeland Security	1	2
Small Business Administration	0	3
State	1	2
Treasury	5	6
Total	1	2

Source: GAO analysis of agency data. I GAO-14-753

The agencies' relatively small increase in cloud spending as a percent of their overall IT budgets, is attributed in part, to the fact that these agencies collectively had not considered cloud computing services for about 67 percent of their investments. With regard to why these investments had not been assessed, the agencies said it was in large part due to these being legacy investments in operations and maintenance; the agencies had only planned to consider cloud options for these investments when they were to be modernized or replaced. This is inconsistent with Office of Management and Budget policy that calls for cloud solutions to be considered first whenever a secure, reliable, and cost-effective option exists regardless of where the investment is in its life cycle. Until the agencies fully assess all their IT investments, they will not be able to achieve the resulting benefits of operational efficiencies and cost savings.

The agencies collectively reported cost savings of about $96 million from the implementation of 22 of the 101 cloud services. These savings included both one-time and multiyear savings. For example, the General Services Administration saved $2.6 million by migrating to a cloud customer service solution, and Homeland Security saved $1.2 million from fiscal years 2011 through 2013 by implementing a cloud-based collaboration service. Agency officials cited two major reasons for why the other services they had implemented did not save money. First, a motivation for changing to some of the cloud-based services was not to reduce spending, but to improve service. Second, in selected cases, the cloud computing service opened up a new service or provided a higher quality of service; while this provided useful benefits to the agency, the associated costs negated any savings.

Contents

Tables

Figure

Abbreviations

CIO	chief information officer
DHS	Department of Homeland Security
FedRAMP	Federal Risk and Authorization Management Program
GSA	General Services Administration
HHS	Department of Health and Human Services
IT	information technology
NIST	National Institute of Standards and Technology
OMB	Office of Management and Budget
SBA	Small Business Administration
State	Department of State
Treasury	Department of the Treasury
USDA	U.S. Department of Agriculture

GAO U.S. GOVERNMENT ACCOUNTABILITY OFFICE

441 G St. N.W.
Washington, DC 20548

September 25, 2014

The Honorable Thomas R. Carper
Chairman
The Honorable Tom Coburn, M.D.
Ranking Member
Committee on Homeland Security and Governmental Affairs
United States Senate

The Honorable Ron Johnson
Ranking Member
Subcommittee on Financial and Contracting Oversight
Committee on Homeland Security and Governmental Affairs
United States Senate

The Honorable Gerald E. Connolly
Ranking Member
Subcommittee on Government Operations
Committee on Oversight and Government Reform
United States House of Representatives

Cloud computing is a relatively new and emerging process for acquiring and delivering computing services via information technology (IT) networks, including the Internet. According to the National Institute of Standards and Technology (NIST), cloud computing is a means for enabling on-demand access to shared and scalable pools of computing resources with the goal of minimizing management effort or service provider interaction. As a result, cloud computing offers potential increased benefits, including faster service and reduced IT costs, compared to traditional IT processes currently being used by federal agencies and others.

To encourage federal agencies to begin taking advantage of cloud computing services, the Office of Management and Budget (OMB) issued guidance in December 2010 on implementing these services.[1] The guidance identified cloud computing as having the potential to play a

---

[1]OMB, *25 Point Implementation Plan to Reform Federal Information Technology Management* (Washington, D.C.: Dec. 9, 2010).

major part in achieving operational efficiencies in the federal government's IT environment, including improving asset use and reducing duplicative systems. To help achieve these efficiencies, OMB developed a "Cloud First" policy[2] (dated February 2011) that required each agency's chief information officer (CIO) to implement a cloud service whenever there was a secure, reliable, cost-effective option. In July 2012, we reported[3] on the status and progress of seven agencies in implementing this new policy.[4]

More recently, you asked us to assess, among other things, the seven agencies' progress in implementing cloud services since our 2012 report. Specifically, our objectives were to (1) assess these selected agencies' progress in using cloud computing services, (2) determine the extent to which the selected agencies have experienced cost savings when such services have been deployed, and (3) identify any challenges the selected agencies are facing as they use cloud computing.

To address our first objective, we selected the same seven agencies[5] that were reported on in 2012 so we could compare any progress made since then. (The agencies were selected using a combination of size of the agency's IT budget and prior experience in using cloud services.) We analyzed documentation from the agencies, including data on the number of and funding for current cloud services and compared this with the results from our 2012 report. In addition, we interviewed agency officials responsible for cloud services to corroborate progress. Further, we reviewed agency data on the extent to which the seven agencies had assessed new and ongoing investments for potential cloud services. We also interviewed OMB officials to understand cloud computing guidance

---

[2]OMB, *Federal Cloud Computing Strategy* (Washington, D.C.: Feb. 8, 2011) and CIO Council and Chief Acquisition Officers Council, *Creating Effective Cloud Computing Contracts for the Federal Government, Best Practices for Acquiring IT as a Service* (Feb. 24, 2012).

[3]See GAO, *Information Technology Reform: Progress Made but Future Cloud Computing Efforts Should be Better Planned*, GAO-12-756 (Washington, D.C.: July 2012).

[4]The selected agencies were the Departments of Agriculture (USDA), Homeland Security (DHS), Health and Human Services (HHS), State (State), and the Treasury (Treasury); the General Services Administration (GSA); and Small Business Administration (SBA).

[5]The Departments of Agriculture, Homeland Security, Health and Human Services, State, and the Treasury; the General Services Administration; and Small Business Administration. In this report, each of the seven will be referred to as an "agency."

for federal agencies. Based on the procedures described, we concluded that the data presented are sufficiently reliable for our purposes.

For the second objective, we analyzed agency cost savings data for each cloud service through fiscal year 2013 and identified any additional benefits. In addition, we analyzed agency documentation and interviewed appropriate officials to (1) corroborate the reported cost savings and cost avoidances and (2) obtain information on other benefits from implemented cloud services. In doing this, we determined that the data were sufficiently reliable for the purpose of this report.

Regarding our third objective, we interviewed officials from each of the selected agencies and asked them to identify challenges associated with implementation of their cloud computing services. We then assessed and categorized the challenges and totaled the number of times each challenge was cited by agency officials. In order to identify the common challenges, we generalized challenges that were mentioned by two or more agencies.

We conducted this performance audit from December 2013 through August 2014 in accordance with generally accepted government auditing standards. Those standards require that we plan and perform the audit to obtain sufficient, appropriate evidence to provide a reasonable basis for our findings and conclusions based on our audit objectives. We believe that the evidence obtained provides a reasonable basis for our findings and conclusions based on our audit objectives. Further details of our objectives, scope, and methodology are included in appendix I.

Background

Over the last 15 years, the federal government's increasing demand for IT has led to a dramatic rise in operational costs to develop, implement, and maintain systems and services. Annually, the federal government spends more than $80 billion on IT. While the use of IT has the potential to greatly improve service for federal employees and American taxpayers, it has also led to federal agencies' reliance on custom IT systems that can—and have—become risky, costly, and unproductive mistakes. As part of a comprehensive effort to increase the operational efficiency of federal IT systems and deliver greater value to taxpayers, federal agencies are being required by OMB to shift their IT services to a cloud computing option when feasible.[6]

Overview of Cloud-based Computing Services

According to NIST, cloud computing is a means "for enabling convenient, on-demand network access to a shared pool of configurable computing resources that can be rapidly provisioned and released with minimal management effort or service provider interaction." NIST also states that an application should possess five essential characteristics to be considered cloud computing: on-demand self service, broad network access, resource pooling, rapid elasticity, and measured service.[7] Essentially, cloud computing applications are network-based and scalable on demand.

According to OMB, cloud computing offers these benefits to federal agencies:

- Economical: cloud computing is a pay-as-you-go approach to IT, in which a low initial investment is required to begin, and additional investment is needed only as system use increases.
- Flexible: IT departments that anticipate fluctuations in user demand no longer need to scramble for additional hardware and software. With cloud computing, they can add or subtract capacity quickly and easily.
- Fast: cloud computing eliminates long procurement and certification processes, while providing a near-limitless selection of services.

According to NIST, cloud computing offers three service models:

- Infrastructure as a service—the service provider delivers and manages the basic computing infrastructure of servers, software, storage, and network equipment on which a platform (i.e., operating

---

[6]OMB, *25 Point Implementation Plan to Reform Federal Information Technology Management* (Washington, D.C.: Dec. 9, 2010).

[7]NIST further defines these characteristics as follows. On-demand self-service allows consumers to acquire computing capabilities automatically and as needed. Broad network access provides capabilities over a network, which is accessed through standard mechanisms (e.g., a mobile phone, tablet, laptop, and workstation). Resource pooling means the vendor's combined computing resources serve multiple consumers. Rapid elasticity refers to the ability to vary resources commensurate with demand. Measured services are incrementally valued, typically on a pay-per-use, or charge-per-use, basis.

system and programming tools and services) to develop and execute applications can be developed by the consumer.

- Platform as a service—the service provider delivers and manages the underlying infrastructure (i.e., servers, software, storage, and network equipment), as well as the platform (i.e., operating system, and programming tools and services) on which the consumer can create applications using programming tools supported by the service provider or other sources.

- Software as a service—the service provider delivers one or more applications and the computational resources and underlying infrastructure to run them for use on demand as a turnkey service.

As can be seen in figure 1, each service model offers unique functionality, with consumer control of the environment decreasing from infrastructure to platform to software.

Figure 1: Cloud Service Provider and Consumer Responsibilities for the Three Service Models

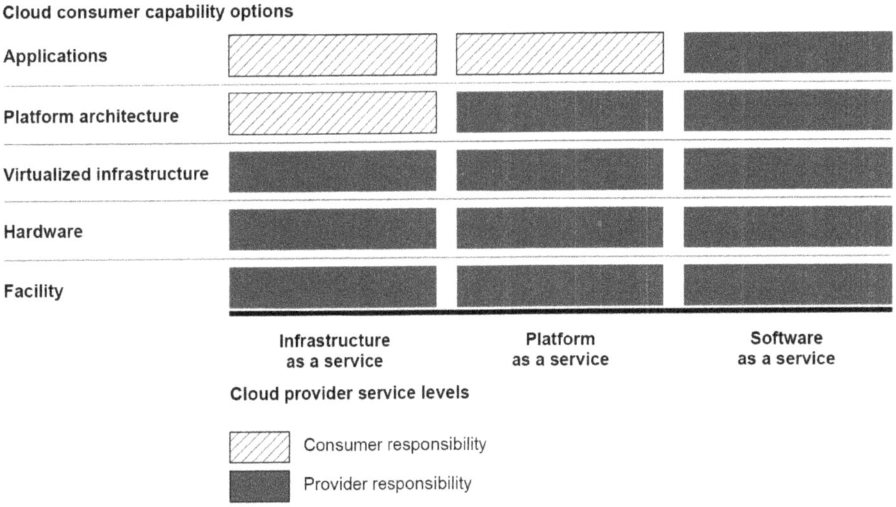

Source: GAO analysis based on National Institute of Standards and Technology. | GAO-14-753

NIST has also defined four deployment models for providing cloud services: private, community, public, and hybrid.

- In a private cloud, the service is set up specifically for one organization, although there may be multiple customers within that organization and the cloud may exist on or off the customer's premises.

- In a community cloud, the service is set up for organizations with similar requirements. The cloud may be managed by the organizations or a third party and may exist on or off the organization's premises.
- A public cloud is available to the general public and is owned and operated by the service provider.
- A hybrid cloud is a composite of two or more of the above deployment models (private, community, or public) that are bound together by standardized or proprietary technology that enables data and application portability.

According to federal guidance, these deployment models determine the number of consumers and the nature of other consumers' data that may be present in a cloud environment. A public cloud should not allow a consumer to know or control other consumers of a cloud service provider's environment. However, a private cloud can allow for ultimate control in selecting who has access to a cloud environment. Community clouds and hybrid clouds allow for a mixed degree of control and knowledge of other consumers. Additionally, the cost for cloud services typically increases as control over other consumers and knowledge of these consumers increase.

OMB Has Issued Guidance for Cloud-based Computing Services

According to OMB, the federal government needs to shift from building custom computer systems to adopting cloud technologies and shared services, which will improve the government's operational efficiencies and result in substantial cost savings. To help agencies achieve these benefits, OMB required agencies to immediately shift to a "Cloud First" policy and increase their use of available cloud-based and shared services whenever a secure, reliable, and cost-effective cloud service exists.

In order to accelerate the adoption of cloud computing services across the government, in December 2010, OMB made cloud computing an integral part of its *25 Point Implementation Plan to Reform Federal*

Information Technology Management.[8] The plan specified six major goals:

- strengthen program management,
- streamline governance and improve accountability,
- increase engagement with industry,
- align the acquisition process with the technology cycle,
- align the budget process with the technology cycle, and
- apply "light technology" and shared services.[9]

To achieve these goals, the plan outlined 25 action items for agencies, such as completing plans to consolidate 800 data centers by 2015[10] and developing a governmentwide strategy to hasten the adoption of cloud computing services. To accelerate the shift, OMB required agencies to identify, plan, and fully migrate three services to a cloud-based one by June 2012.[11]

In February 2011, OMB issued the *Federal Cloud Computing Strategy*,[12] as called for in its 25-Point Plan. The strategy provided definitions of cloud computing services; benefits of cloud services, such as accelerating data center consolidations; a decision framework for migrating services to a cloud environment;[13] case studies to support agencies' migration to cloud computing services; and roles and responsibilities for federal agencies. For example, the strategy states that NIST's role is to lead and collaborate with federal, state, and local government agency chief information officers, private sector experts, and international bodies to identify standards and guidance and prioritize the adoption of cloud computing services.

---

[8]OMB, *25 Point Implementation Plan to Reform Federal Information Technology Management* (Washington, D.C.: Dec. 9, 2010).

[9]According to OMB, "light technologies" are cloud services.

[10]As of December 2011, OMB planned for agencies to consolidate 1,200 data centers by 2015.

[11]See, GAO-12-756.

[12]OMB, *Federal Cloud Computing Strategy* (Washington, D.C.: Feb. 8, 2011).

[13]The decision framework, among other things, identifies several key areas for determining the readiness for moving to a cloud environment, including the ability of the cloud service provider to address government security requirements.

In a December 2011 memo, OMB established the Federal Risk and Authorization Management Program (FedRAMP),[14] a governmentwide program to provide joint authorizations and continuous security monitoring services for cloud computing services for all federal agencies. Among other things, the memo required the General Services Administration (GSA) to issue a concept of operations,[15] which was completed in February 2012. The concept of operations states that FedRAMP is to:

- ensure that cloud computing services have adequate information security;
- eliminate duplication of effort and reduce risk management costs; and
- enable rapid and cost-effective procurement of information systems/services for federal agencies.

GSA initiated FedRAMP operations, which the agency referred to as initial operational capabilities, in June 2012.

Prior GAO Work Identified Progress and Improvements Needed in Implementing Cloud-based Computing Services

We have previously reported on federal agencies' efforts to implement cloud computing services, and on progress oversight agencies have made to help federal agencies in those efforts. These include:

- In May 2010, we reported on the efforts of multiple agencies to ensure the security of governmentwide cloud computing services.[16] We noted that, while OMB, GSA, and NIST had initiated efforts to ensure secure cloud computing services, OMB had not yet finished a cloud computing strategy; GSA had begun a procurement for expanding cloud computing services, but had not yet developed specific plans for establishing a shared information security assessment and authorization process; and NIST had not yet issued cloud-specific security guidance. We recommended that OMB establish milestones to complete a strategy for federal cloud computing and ensure it

[14]OMB, *Security Authorization of Information Systems in Cloud Computing Environments* (Washington, D.C.: Dec. 8, 2011). FedRAMP is governed by the Joint Authorization Board (composed of the CIOs from the Departments of Defense and Homeland Security, and GSA), the FedRAMP program management office, NIST, the Federal CIO Council, OMB, and the Department of Homeland Security.

[15]GSA, *FedRAMP Concept of Operations* (CONOPS) version 1.0 (Washington, D.C.: Feb. 7, 2012).

[16]GAO, *Information Security: Federal Guidance Needed to Address Control Issues with Implementing Cloud Computing*, GAO-10-513 (Washington, D.C.: May 27, 2010).

addressed information security challenges. These include having a process to assess vendor compliance with government information security requirements and division of information security responsibilities between the customer and vendor. OMB agreed with our recommendations and subsequently published a strategy in February 2011 that addressed the importance of information security when using cloud computing, but it did not fully address several key challenges confronting agencies, such as the appropriate use of attestation standards for control assessments of cloud computing service providers, and division of information security-related responsibilities between customer and provider. We also recommended that GSA consider security in its procurement for cloud services, including consideration of a shared assessment and authorization process. GSA generally agreed with our recommendations and has since developed its FedRAMP program, an assessment and authorization process for systems shared among federal agencies. Finally, we recommended that NIST issue guidance specific to cloud-based computing security. NIST agreed with our recommendations and has since issued multiple publications that address such guidance.

- In April 2012, we reported that more needed to be done to implement OMB's 25-Point Plan and measure its results.[17] Among other things, we reported that, of the 10 key action items that we reviewed, 3 had been completed and 7 had been partially completed by December 2011. In particular, OMB and agencies' cloud-related efforts only partially addressed requirements. Specifically, agencies' plans were missing key elements, such as a discussion of needed resources, a migration schedule, and plans for retiring legacy systems. As a result, we recommended, among other things, that the Secretaries of Homeland Security and Veterans Affairs, and the Attorney General direct their respective CIOs to complete elements missing from the agencies' plans for migrating services to a cloud computing environment. Officials from each of the agencies generally agreed with our recommendations and have taken steps to implement them.

- In July 2012, we reported that the seven federal agencies we reviewed had made progress in meeting OMB's requirement to

---

[17]GAO, *Information Technology Reform: Progress Made; More Needs to Be Done to Complete Actions and Measure Results*, GAO-12-461 (Washington, D.C.: Apr. 26, 2012).

implement three cloud computing services by June 2012.[18] Specifically, the seven agencies had implemented 21 cloud computing services and spent a total of $307 million for cloud computing in fiscal year 2012, about 1 percent of their total IT budgets. However, two agencies reported that they did not have plans to meet OMB's deadline to implement three services by June 2012, but would do so by calendar year's end. Agencies also shared seven common challenges that they experienced in moving services to cloud computing. The seven challenges included:

- **Meeting federal security requirements**: Cloud service vendors may not be familiar with security requirements that are unique to government agencies, such as continuous monitoring and maintaining an inventory of systems.

- **Obtaining guidance**: Existing federal guidance for using cloud services may be insufficient or incomplete. Agencies cited a number of areas where additional guidance is needed, such as purchasing commodity IT and assessing Federal Information Security Management Act[19] security levels.

- **Acquiring knowledge and expertise**: Agencies may not have the necessary tools or resources, such as expertise among staff, to implement cloud services.

- **Certifying and accrediting vendors**: Agencies may not have a mechanism for certifying that vendors meet standards for security, in part because FedRAMP had not yet been made operational (i.e., reached initial operating capabilities).

- **Ensuring data portability and interoperability:** To preserve their ability to change vendors in the future, agencies may attempt to avoid platforms or technologies that "lock" customers into a particular product.

---

[18]GAO-12-756.

[19]NIST guidance, required under the *Federal Information Security Management Act of 2002*, defines three levels of potential impact on organizations or individuals should there be a breach of security (i.e., a loss of confidentiality, integrity, or availability). The three potential impact levels of a breach are: low (limited adverse effect), moderate (serious adverse effect), and high (catastrophic adverse effect).

- **Overcoming cultural barriers**: Agency culture may act as an obstacle to implementing cloud services.

- **Procuring services on a consumption (on-demand) basis:** Because of the on-demand, scalable nature of cloud services, it can be difficult to define specific quantities and costs. These uncertainties make contracting and budgeting difficult due to the fluctuating costs associated with scalable and incremental cloud service procurements.

While each of the seven agencies had submitted plans to OMB for implementing their cloud services, a majority of the plans were missing required elements. Agencies have also identified opportunities for future cloud service implementations, such as moving storage and help desk services to a cloud environment. We made recommendations to seven agencies to develop planning information, such as estimated costs and legacy IT systems' retirement plans for existing and planned services. The agencies generally agreed with our recommendations and have taken actions to implement them.

Agencies Have Made Progress in Implementing Cloud Computing Services, but Progress Is Uneven

OMB's *Cloud First* policy requires federal agencies to implement cloud computing services whenever a secure, reliable, and cost-effective cloud option exists. In July 2012, we found that all of the seven agencies had among other things, identified at least three services to implement in a cloud environment, and all but two had implemented three cloud computing services.

Since then, the agencies have added more cloud computing services. In total, the number of cloud computing services implemented increased from 21 to 101, an increase of 80 services. Table 1 lists the number of cloud computing services implemented by each agency in 2012 and 2014.

Table 1: Number of Cloud Computing Services Implemented by Agency as of July 2012 and July 2014

Agency	Number of cloud computing services implemented as of July 2012	Number of cloud computing services implemented as of July 2014	Increase in number of cloud computing services
DHS	6	11	5 (83%)
GSA	3	21	18 (600%)
HHS	3	36	33 (1100%)
SBA	1	4	3 (300%)
State	3	14	11 (367%)
Treasury	3	5	2 (67%)
USDA	2	10	8 (400%)
Total	**21**	**101**	**80 (381%)**

Source: GAO analysis of agency data. | GAO-14-753

While the number of cloud computing services increased by 80 since 2012, the number implemented by each agency during that time varied. For example, since 2012, HHS had implemented 33 such services, while SBA, State, and Treasury had implemented 3, 11, and 2, respectively. (A brief description of the 101 cloud computing services implemented by each agency is included in app. II.)

These agencies also increased the amount they budgeted and reported spending on cloud computing services. Specifically, the seven agencies, collectively, reported their spending increased by $222 million, from $307 million to $529 million. Table 2 shows the amount each agency (1) reported spending on cloud computing services in fiscal year 2012 and (2) planned to spend in fiscal year 2014.

Table 2: Amount Reported Spent for Cloud Computing Services for Fiscal Year 2012 and Budgeted for Fiscal Year 2014 (in millions of dollars)

Agency	Amount reported spent on cloud computing services in fiscal year 2012	Amount budgeted for cloud computing services in fiscal year 2014	Increase in amount for cloud computing services
DHS	$74	$109	$35 (47%)
GSA	13	30	17 (131%)
HHS	26	64	38 (146%)
SBA	0	3	3 (*[a])
State	11	32	21 (191%)
Treasury	165	202	37 (22%)
USDA	18	89	71 (394%)
Total	**$307**	**$529**	**$222 (72%)**

Source: GAO analysis of agency data. | GAO-14-753

[a] Percentage increase is not calculable.

Although collectively the amount budgeted in 2014 by the agencies ($529 million) is an overall increase of 72 percent, the amounts and percentages varied significantly across the agencies. For example, USDA increased its planned cloud spending by $71 million (a 394 percent change over 2012), while Treasury budgeted $37 million more (a 22 percent increase over 2012).

Further, the agencies also increased the collective percentage of their IT budgets allocated to cloud computing services. Specifically, as shown in table 3, the agencies collectively doubled the percentage of their IT budgets from 1 to 2 percent during the fiscal year 2012 -14 period. However, on an individual agency basis, the percentage increase varied. For example, GSA increased the percentage of its IT budget allocated to cloud computing from 2 to 5 percent while DHS increased its allocation from 1 to 2 percent.

Even though the agencies collectively and individually increased the percentage of their IT budgets allocated to cloud services, our analysis showed that the agencies are still devoting a large portion of their IT budgets to non-cloud computing expenditures. Specifically, as shown in table 3, the agencies in 2014 were collectively budgeting 2 percent of their IT budgets to cloud services, while the remaining 98 percent were dedicated to non-cloud expenditures.

Table 3: Amount for Cloud Computing Services for Fiscal Years 2012 and 2014

Agency	Percent of IT budget reported spent on cloud computing services in fiscal year 2012	Total amount reported spent on cloud computing services (millions) /IT budget fiscal year 2012 (billions)	Percent budgeted for cloud computing services in fiscal year 2014	Total amount budgeted for cloud computing services (millions) /IT budget fiscal year 2014 (billions)
DHS	1%	$74/5.6	2%	$109/5.8
GSA	2%	13/.537	5%	30/.593
HHS	0%	26/7.2	1%	64/7.3
SBA	0%	0/.102	3%	3/.102
State	1%	11/1.4	2%	32/1.4
Treasury	5%	165/3.4	6%	202/3.5
USDA	1%	18/2.5	3%	89/2.6
Total	**1%**	**307/20.7**	**2%**	**529/21.3**

Source: GAO analysis of agency data. I GAO-14-753

Officials from OMB and the agencies attributed the agencies' varying degrees of progress in part, to the following: in implementing its Cloud First policy, OMB has granted the agencies discretion in determining whether and which services are to be migrated. Specifically, officials from OMB's Office of E-Government & Information Technology told us that they initially had established goals for the agencies but instead granted them the latitude to annually assess all their investments and identify those investments that were appropriate for their agency to migrate. As a result, some agencies have been more aggressive than others in moving services to the cloud.

In addition, the agencies' relatively low percentage of budget allocated to cloud spending is due in large part to the fact that the agencies have not assessed a majority of their investments, although OMB's guidance calls for agencies to assess all their IT services for migration to the cloud irrespective of where each investment is in its life cycle. Specifically, as shown in table 4, the agencies collectively had not assessed about 67 percent of their 2000 investments. Table 4 provides further detail on the number of investments in fiscal year 2014 that were chosen for cloud computing services; the number of investments that were evaluated for cloud computing services, but an alternative was chosen; and the number not evaluated for cloud computing services.

Table 4: Number of Investments in Fiscal Year 2014 that Were Chosen for Cloud Computing Services; Number that Were Evaluated for Cloud Services, but Another Alternative Was Chosen; and the Number Not Evaluated for Cloud Services

Agency	Evaluated and chosen for cloud computing services	Evaluated for cloud services but another alternative was chosen	Not evaluated for cloud services	Total
DHS	47	24	282	353
GSA	18	33	37	88
HHS	70	205	601	876
SBA	4	5	29	38
State	8	11	56	75
Treasury	47	83	189	319
USDA	51	49	151	251
Total	**245 (12%)**	**410 (21%)**	**1345 (67%)**	**2000**

Source: GAO analysis of agency data. I GAO-14-753

A key reason cited by the agency officials for why most of their investments had not been evaluated for cloud services was that they were largely legacy investments in operations and maintenance; the agencies had only planned to consider cloud options when the investments were to be modernized or replaced at the end of their life cycle. Agency officials added that it was a challenge to assess and ultimately replace such legacy systems because agency personnel were often reluctant to cede direct control of mission-critical IT resources. While we recognize the cultural challenge to moving investments to the cloud (which is discussed in more detail later in this report), OMB guidance nonetheless calls for agencies to continually assess all investments irrespective of where they are in their life cycle. Agency officials were aware of the OMB guidance and said they had plans to assess their unevaluated investments in the near future. Nevertheless, the agencies for the most part were not able to provide us with specific dates for when assessments of these investments were to be performed. Establishing such milestones is an important management tool to ensuring policy outcomes—including those envisioned by OMB's cloud policy—are achieved in an efficient and effective manner.[20]

---

[20]See, for example, GAO, *The Standards for Internal Control in the Federal Government*, GAO/AIMD-00-21.3.1 (Washington, D.C.: November 1999).

Until the agencies assess their IT investments that have yet to be evaluated for suitability for migration to the cloud, they will not know which services are likely candidates for migration to cloud computing services, and therefore will not gain the operational efficiencies and cost savings associated with using such services.

Agencies Reported Cost Savings from Implementation of Cloud Computing Services

Agencies reported that they had cost savings[21] from implementing 22 out of 101 cloud computing services through fiscal year 2013. Specifically, they collectively saved about $96 million by implementing these 22 services. Table 5 lists the total number of cloud computing services reported by each agency, the number of cloud services with cost savings, and the total savings.

Table 5: Reported Cost Savings from Implementation of Cloud Computing Services

Agency	Total number of cloud computing services	Number of cloud computing services with cost savings (in percentage)	Cost savings (in millions)
DHS	11	5 (45%)	$34.10
GSA	21	4 (19%)	16.18
HHS	36	4 (11%)	1.19
SBA	4	2 (50%)	.30
State	14	2 (14%)	1.28
Treasury	5	2 (40%)	7.30
USDA	10	3 (30%)	35.60
Total	101	22 (22%)	$95.95

Source: GAO analysis of agency data. I GAO-14-753

These savings included both one-time savings and life-cycle savings. For example, GSA had a one-time cost savings of $2.6 million by migrating to a cloud customer service solution, which was a less expensive alternative than upgrading its existing system. DHS had a cumulate savings of $1.2 million through fiscal year 2013 for its collaboration platform that is used to build applications and manage documents, which was implemented in fiscal year 2011.

---

[21]In this report, cost savings includes both cost savings and cost avoidances. According to OMB, cost savings are a reduction in actual expenditures below the projected level of costs to achieve a specific objective. Cost avoidance is an action taken in the immediate time frame that will decrease costs in the future.

According to agency officials, two major factors governed why the remaining services (79) did not achieve savings. First, a motivation for changing to some of the cloud-based services was not to reduce spending, but to improve service. Second, in selected cases, the cloud computing service opened up a new service or provided a higher quality of service; while this provided useful benefits to the agency, the associated costs negated any savings.

In addition to these cost savings, agency officials identified the following benefits from migrating systems and services to a cloud computing service.

- **Decreased time to deploy**: A cloud computing service can be deployed more quickly and migrating a system to a cloud allows an agency to run it for a short period of time and then shut it down, without having to develop a unique infrastructure for it.
- **Increased flexibility**: Cloud computing services are useful for systems that have varying use throughout a year, as the cloud service can be easily scaled up when there is high demand.
- **Reduced IT infrastructure:** Implementation of cloud computing services reduces the amount of IT infrastructure required onsite, in particular, data center resources.

Agencies Continue to Experience Challenges in Implementing Cloud Computing Services

Officials from the agencies we reviewed cited five challenges they have experienced in implementing cloud computing services. Of the five, two challenges—meeting federal security requirements and overcoming cultural barriers—were previously identified and discussed in our 2012 report.[22]

According to the officials, meeting federal security requirements was a continuing challenge because the requirements for new services are a moving target (i.e., the requirements are regularly being updated to address new threats, vulnerabilities, and technologies, and vendors may not be able to meet them). For example, NIST recently made revisions to its cloud security requirements and agencies are still in the process of getting familiar with them. As a result, agencies fear making mistakes that could negatively impact the security of systems and data. With regard to overcoming cultural barriers, DHS officials said that shifting to a new

---

[22]GAO-12-756.

business model from a legacy business model requires cultural change, which continues to be a challenge at the department. In addition, GSA officials said that, as they move the management of servers and software off site, a continuing challenge is getting agency staff to adapt to an operational environment where they do not have direct control and access to agency IT resources.

In addition to the two challenges repeated from 2012, officials reported these three new challenges.

- **Meeting new network infrastructure requirements.** Current network infrastructure, topology (network configuration), or bandwidth (data transmission rate) is often insufficient to meet new infrastructure needs when agencies transition to cloud computing services. For example, officials at State said that legacy systems with a particular infrastructure designed to meet certain federal requirements will need to be reengineered to work in a multi-tiered cloud environment. USDA officials stated that they would need to consider redesigning their network topology to accommodate new cloud service bandwidth requirements and traffic streams.

- **Having appropriate expertise for acquisition processes.** Migrating legacy systems to cloud computing services requires knowledgeable acquisition staff and appropriate processes. For example, HHS officials stated that while the department has the capability to purchase cloud services, it has found post award management to be a challenge. These officials added that to respond to this challenge, HHS is working with its personnel as well as other stakeholders, such as GSA, to develop best practices for cloud post award management and related acquisition activities. In addition, DHS officials said that efforts to transition from legacy systems to cloud computing services require streamlining their IT services supply chain, which requires an evaluation of the component processes and time to fully implement this transformation.

- **Funding for implementation.** Funding for the initial implementation of a cloud service can be a significant cost to agencies. For example, officials at State said that the cost of migrating an application to a cloud service poses a challenge in the current budget environment where IT budgets are declining. In addition, GSA officials stated that initial implementation requires additional funding that has not been made available.

While these challenges are formidable, OMB and GSA have provided guidance and services to help agencies address many of these challenges. For example, GSA developed FedRAMP, which is a program to create processes for security authorizations and allow agencies to leverage security authorizations on a governmentwide basis in an effort to streamline the certification and accreditation process. GSA also provides continuous monitoring services for cloud computing services for all federal agencies.

In addition, OMB's *Federal Cloud Computing Strategy*[23] addresses how agencies can overcome redesign and implementation challenges. In particular, the strategy states that agencies should ensure that their network infrastructure can support the demand for higher bandwidth before migrating to a cloud service. The strategy also directs agencies to assess readiness for migration to a cloud service by determining the suitability of the existing legacy application and data to either migrate to the cloud service (i.e., rehost an application in a cloud environment) or be replaced by a cloud service (i.e., retire the legacy system and replace with a commercial equivalent).

Further, GSA provides services to assist agencies with procuring and acquiring cloud services. Specifically, GSA established contracts that the agencies can use to obtain commodity services such as cloud infrastructure as a service and cloud e-mail; these contracts—which were established in October 2010 and September 2012, respectively—are intended to reduce the burden on agencies for the most common IT services. GSA also created working groups to support commodity service migration by developing technical requirements for shared services to reduce the analytical burden on individual government agencies.

Regarding funding, the strategy recommends that agencies reevaluate their technology sourcing strategy to include consideration and application of cloud computing services as part of their budget process.

Officials stated that they consult the *Federal Cloud Computing Strategy* to guide them in their efforts to move services to the cloud. For example, SBA officials said that they consult this guidance as they plan for and prepare to move services to the cloud. In addition, State officials said that

---

[23]OMB, *Federal Cloud Computing Strategy* (Washington, D.C.: Feb. 8, 2011).

they use the strategy as part of their process to prepare them in their efforts to consider cloud services.

Conclusions

Since we last reported on these seven agencies, they have made varying degrees of progress in implementing cloud computing services, and in doing so, have saved money and realized other benefits. While the collective and individual agency gains in implementing such services are commendable, the seven agencies are still only investing a small fraction of their IT budgets on cloud computing. The agencies' modest level of cloud investment is attributable in part to the large number of legacy investments—nearly two thirds of all investments—that have yet to be considered for cloud migration. This is due in part to the agencies' practice of not assessing these investments until they are to be replaced or modernized, which is inconsistent with OMB's direction. Nonetheless, the large number of agency investments to be assessed provides ample opportunities for additional progress and substantial cost savings. An important step to realizing this progress and savings is ensuring these investments are assessed, which includes establishing milestones for when the assessments are to be performed. Until this is done and the investments are assessed, the agencies cannot know whether they are achieving the maximum benefits, including improved operational efficiencies and minimized costs, associated with using such services.

Agencies continue to face formidable challenges as they move their IT services to the cloud. Two of the challenges—namely ensuring IT security and overcoming agency culture—have persisted since we last reported. OMB and GSA have issued guidance and established initiatives to address the challenges, which agencies can use to help mitigate any associated negative impacts.

Recommendation for Executive Action

To help ensure continued progress in the implementation of cloud computing services, we recommend that the Secretaries of Agriculture, Health and Human Services, Homeland Security, State, and the Treasury; and the Administrators of the General Services Administration and Small Business Administration direct their respective Chief Information Officers to take the following actions:

- Ensure that all IT investments are assessed for suitability for migration to a cloud computing service.

- As part of this, establish evaluation dates for those investments identified in this report that have not been assessed for migration to the cloud.

Agency Comments and Our Evaluation

In commenting on a draft of this report, six agencies—DHS, GSA, HHS, SBA, State, and USDA—agreed with our recommendations, and one agency (Treasury) had no comments. The specific comments from each agency are as follows:

- DHS, in its written comments—which are reprinted in appendix III—stated that it concurred with our recommendations. The department also provided technical comments, which we have incorporated in the report as appropriate.

- In its written comments, GSA stated it agreed with our findings and recommendations and will take appropriate action. GSA's comments are reprinted in appendix IV.

- HHS, in comments provided via e-mail from its Audit Liaison within the Office of the Assistant Secretary for Legislation, stated it concurred with our recommendations. The department also provided technical comments, which we have incorporated in the report as appropriate.

- SBA, in comments provided via e-mail from its Program Manager within the Office of Congressional and Legislative Affairs, stated that it concurred with our report. It also commented that of the 29 investments that SBA did not evaluate for cloud computing (identified in table 4), only 17 could be evaluated for cloud alternatives. SBA said the other 12 investments cannot be considered for a cloud alternative, but provided no documentation to support this statement.

- USDA, in comments provided via an e-mail from its GAO Agency Liaison within the Office of the Chief Information Officer, stated that it agreed with our recommendations and is committed to implementing OMB's Cloud First policy.

- State, in its written comments (which are reprinted in appendix V), noted that it had already addressed our recommendations. Specifically, the department said it developed and communicated guidance to its IT investment owners on how to implement OMB's Cloud First policy and that all investments are currently undergoing cloud computing alternatives analyses with the goal of having these assessments completed by the end of calendar year 2014. State also provided technical comments, which we have incorporated in the report as appropriate.

- Treasury, in its written comments, stated that the department had no comments on the report and appreciated our efforts in developing it. Treasury's written comments are reprinted in appendix VI.

We are sending copies of this report to interested congressional committees; the Secretaries of Agriculture, Health and Human Services, Homeland Security, State, and the Treasury; the Administrator of the General Services Administration and Small Business Administration; the Director of the Office of Management and Budget: and other interested parties. This report will also be available at no charge on our website at http://www.gao.gov.

If you or your staffs have any questions on matters discussed in this report, please contact me at (202) 512-9286 or pownerd@gao.gov. Contact points for our Offices of Congressional Relations and Public Affairs may be found on the last page of this report. GAO staff who made major contributions to this report are listed in appendix VII.

David A. Powner
Director
Information Technology Management Issues

Appendix I: Objectives, Scope, and Methodology

Our engagement objectives were to (1) assess selected agencies' progress in using cloud computing services, (2) determine the extent to which selected agencies have experienced cost savings when such services have been deployed, and (3) identify any challenges selected agencies are facing as they use cloud computing.

To address our first objective, we selected the same seven agencies that were selected for our 2012 review so that we could compare the progress they have made.[1] The seven agencies selected were the Departments of Agriculture (USDA), Health and Human Services (HHS), Homeland Security (DHS), State, and the Treasury (Treasury); and the General Services Administration (GSA) and Small Business Administration (SBA).

We analyzed budget and related documentation from the selected agencies, including data on the number of and funding for current cloud computing services and compared this information with our previous findings. In addition, we interviewed officials responsible for cloud services to corroborate progress. Further, we reviewed agency data on the extent to which they assessed new and ongoing investments for potential cloud computing services. We also interviewed OMB officials to understand cloud computing guidance for federal agencies. Based on the procedures described, we concluded that the data presented are sufficiently reliable for our purposes.

To address our second objective, we analyzed agency data on cost savings and avoidances through fiscal year 2013 for those cloud services the agencies had implemented. We also interviewed agency officials to obtain information on other benefits the agencies had gained from adopting cloud-based services. To determine the reliability of the data on cost savings and avoidances, we analyzed agency documentation and interviewed appropriate officials to corroborate the cost savings and cost avoidances. We determined that the data were sufficiently reliable for the purpose of this report, which was to identify the extent to which agencies had experienced cost savings for implemented cloud services.

To address the third objective, we interviewed officials from each of the selected agencies and asked them to identify challenges associated with

---

[1]GAO-12-756. The agencies were selected using a combination of size of the agency's IT budget and prior experience in using cloud services.

their implementation of cloud services. We then assessed and
categorized the challenges and totaled the number of times each
challenge was cited by agency officials. In order to identify the common
challenges, we generalized challenges that were mentioned by two or
more agencies. We also compared these challenges with the challenges
that agencies reported in our 2012 review.

In addition, we conducted a content analysis of the information we
received in order to identify and categorize common challenges. To do
so, three team analysts independently reviewed and drafted a series of
challenge statements based on each agency's records. They then worked
together to resolve any discrepancies, choosing to report on challenges
that were identified by two or more agencies. These common challenges
were presented in the report. We also interviewed agency officials to
corroborate the challenges identified.

We conducted this performance audit from December 2013 through
August 2014 in accordance with generally accepted government auditing
standards. Those standards require that we plan and perform the audit to
obtain sufficient, appropriate evidence to provide a reasonable basis for
our findings and conclusions based on our audit objectives. We believe
that the evidence obtained provides a reasonable basis for our findings
and conclusions based on our audit objectives.

Appendix II: Brief Description of Cloud Computing Services Implemented by Seven Agencies Reviewed (as of July 2014)

This appendix lists the cloud computing services implemented the seven agencies we reviewed; namely, the Departments of Agriculture (USDA), Health and Human Services (HHS), Homeland Security (DHS), State, and the Treasury (Treasury); and the General Services Administration (GSA) and Small Business Administration (SBA). It also includes as reported by the agencies, a description of each service to be provided, the service model, deployment model, and whether the cloud service is approved/compliant with the Federal Risk and Authorization Management Program (FedRAMP).

DHS

Cloud computing service	Description of service to be provided	Service model[a]	Deployment model[b]	FedRAMP approved/compliant?[c]
E-mail as a Service	Provide the infrastructure for the department's enterprisewide e-mail and calendar functions.	Software	private	no[d]
Workplace as a Service	Enable DHS users to have virtual access to department desktop operating systems and applications anywhere in the world.	Infrastructure	private	yes
Development and Test as a Service	Support DHS's secure information technology (IT) development, test, and preproduction environment that mirrors the production environment. It also is to provide access to a suite of application life-cycle management and automated testing services.	Infrastructure	private	yes
Enterprise Content Delivery as a Service	Ensure that DHS's public-facing websites are always available. DHS adopted this service to protect against denial of service attacks, help manage surge requirements, and reduce hosting costs.	Platform	public	yes
SharePoint as a Service	Provide a secure platform that is to be used by DHS to build applications and manage documents. It also is to provide file management, user collaboration, and workflow routing capabilities.	Platform	private	no[d]
Production as a Service	Enable DHS with rapid provisioning in a secure virtual operating environment and furnish hosting for applications and services, including operating systems, network, and storage.	Infrastructure	private	yes
Project Server as a Service	Provide components with access to a website that allows for the consolidation of projects.	Platform	private	no[d]

Cloud computing service	Description of service to be provided	Service model[a]	Deployment model[b]	FedRAMP approved/compliant?[c]
Case and Relationship Management as a Service	Allow department users to manage customer relationships and enable the user to make informed decisions and followup.	Platform	private	no[d]
Business Intelligence as a Service	Provide DHS with decision-making information and promotes virtual consolidation by integrating business intelligence dashboards.	Platform	private	no
Web Content Management as a Service	Support all of the department's public websites and provides software accessible through the public cloud.	Platform	public	yes
Identity Proofing as a Service	Provide individuals in the United States with a capability to check their employment eligibility status before formally seeking employment.	Platform	public	no

Source: GAO analysis of Department of Homeland Security data. I GAO 14 753

[a]According to the National Institute of Standards and Technology (NIST), cloud computing offers three models describing the type of IT service to be provided; they include; software as a service, platform as a service, and infrastructure as a service. For infrastructure as a service, the service provider delivers and manages the basic computing infrastructure of servers, software, storage, and network equipment on which a platform (i.e., operating system and programming tools and services) to develop and execute applications can be developed by the consumer. For platform as a service, the service provider delivers and manages the underlying infrastructure, as well as the platform on which the consumer can create applications using programming tools supported by the service provider or other sources. For software as a service, the service provider delivers one or more applications and the computational resources and underlying infrastructure to run them for use on demand as a turnkey service.

[b]NIST has defined four models for how cloud services can be deployed; they are: private, community, public, and hybrid. In a private cloud, the service is set up specifically for one organization, although there may be multiple customers within that organization and the cloud may exist on or off the customer's premises. In a community cloud, the service is set up for organizations with similar requirements. The cloud may be managed by the organizations or a third party and may exist on or off the organization's premises. A public cloud is available to the general public and is owned and operated by the service provider. A hybrid cloud is a composite of two or more of the above deployment models (private, community, or public) that are bound together by standardized or proprietary technology that enables data and application portability.

[c]FedRAMP is a governmentwide program initiated by the Office of Management and Budget to provide joint authorizations and continuous security monitoring services for cloud computing services. FedRAMP is intended to (1) ensure that cloud computing services have adequate information security; (2) eliminate duplication of effort and reduce risk management costs; and (3) enable rapid and cost-effective procurement of information systems/services for federal agencies.

[d]DHS reported this service as not being FedRAMP approved/compliant and said it did not need to be so because the service required a higher level of security—which DHS referred to as a Federal Information Security Management Act high baseline—than that provided by FedRAMP.

GSA

Cloud computing service	Description of service to be provided	Service model[a]	Deployment model[b]	FedRAMP approved/compliant?[c]
Acquisition Planning Module	Provide a collaborative on-line platform for GSA to expedite acquisition planning with greater efficiency and effectiveness. Specifically, it is to enable routing of acquisition documents, online collaborative writing capabilities, and automated filing of acquisition plans.	Software	government community	no
Cloud Modernization	Provide a website and services that assist federal agencies in various aspects of implementing cloud services, including integration, migration, business intelligence, data management, analysis, and delivery. The platform is to be hosted by GSA's Office of Citizen Services and Innovative Technology and available for use by all federal agencies.	Infrastructure	government community	no
Data.gov	Provide a platform to enable public access to data, tools, and other resources supplied by federal, state, and local governments, which can be used to conduct research, build applications, and design data visualizations.	Platform	public, community	no
Electronic Capital Planning and Investment Control	Maintain a web-based, government-owned technology service that automates capital planning and portfolio management practices for the department.	Software	government community	yes
Electronic Program Management	Provide a web-based tool that creates a collaborative work environment for GSA-sponsored design and construction projects.	Software	private	yes
Enterprise Service Oriented Architecture	Provide web services that support GSA's Federal Acquisition Service and Public Buildings Service applications.	Infrastructure	public, community	yes
Federal Acquisition Services Salesforce Instance	Allow support for the automation of business processes as well as customer relation management-type activities performed by GSA's Federal Acquisition Service.	Platform, Software	public	no
FBOpen	Maintain an open application server, data import tools, and sample applications to help small businesses search for contracting opportunities with the federal government.	Platform, Software	government community	no

Cloud computing service	Description of service to be provided	Service model[a]	Deployment model[b]	FedRAMP approved/compliant?[c]
Fiberlink	Remove sensitive information from lost or stolen Windows-based government computing equipment for the department. It also is to provide continuous security monitoring.	Software	public	no
Google Apps Services	Provide a cloud-based service for the department for filtering e-mail for unsolicited messages, malware, and content, as well as e-mail archiving and retrieval.	Platform, Software	government community	no
GSA e-mail and Collaboration Solution	Provide GSA staff and onsite contractors with e-mail and office functions--such as documents, spreadsheets, presentations, drawings, and forms--to be used and accessed via desktops, laptops, and mobile devices, including personally owned devices. It also is to provide instant messaging.	Software	private	no
Meeting Space	Enable remote collaborative capabilities for GSA meetings and training.	Platform, Software	private	no
MyUSA	Provide a platform for a federal web site that is to help the public find information and services provided by the federal government. Its goal is to save people and businesses time when transacting with the federal government, increase awareness of available federal services, and speed up notifications and updates.	Infrastructure	government community	no
National Computerized Maintenance and Monitoring System	Consolidate GSA's Public Building Service's computerized maintenance and monitoring systems to a single cloud-based service.	Software	private	no
Public Buildings Service SalesForce Instance	Provide a platform to support the automation of business processes as well as customer relations management type activities performed by GSA's Public Building Service.	Platform, Software	public	no
Performance Management Data Warehouse	Enable a platform capable of hosting, among other things, data warehouses both within a federal agency as well as between federal agencies.	Infrastructure, Platform	private	yes
Prices Paid Portal	Maintain an application to be used by federal agencies to compare prices other agencies have paid for goods and services.	Infrastructure	public, community	yes

GAO-14-753 Cloud Computing

Cloud computing service	Description of service to be provided	Service model[a]	Deployment model[b]	FedRAMP approved/compliant?[c]
SalesForce	Provide a platform for collaboration and customer relationship management application hosting services. It enables employees to, among other things, track customer orders, budget, and perform other customer relationship management activities.	Platform	public	no
Service Now	Provide IT service management tools which automate industry best practices for request, incident, problem, change, configuration, and knowledge management. Offers a service catalog for GSA employees to request IT services.	Platform	private, community	no
The National Alert and Accountability System	Enable mass notification of GSA employees during times of national crisis, regional emergencies, or natural disasters. The system also is designed to allow GSA leadership to communicate with and gain accountability of displaced staff via multiple means.	Software	private	no
USA.gov	Operate a portal for the public to get federal government information and services via the web.	Platform, Software	government community	yes

Source: GAO analysis of General Services Administration data. I GAO-14-753

[a]According to the National Institute of Standards and Technology (NIST), cloud computing offers three models describing the type of IT service to be provided; they include; software as a service, platform as a service, and infrastructure as a service. For infrastructure as a service, the service provider delivers and manages the basic computing infrastructure of servers, software, storage, and network equipment on which a platform (i.e., operating system and programming tools and services) to develop and execute applications can be developed by the consumer. For platform as a service, the service provider delivers and manages the underlying infrastructure, as well as the platform on which the consumer can create applications using programming tools supported by the service provider or other sources. For software as a service, the service provider delivers one or more applications and the computational resources and underlying infrastructure to run them for use on demand as a turnkey service.

[b]NIST has defined four models for how cloud services can be deployed; they are: private, community, public, and hybrid. In a private cloud, the service is set up specifically for one organization, although there may be multiple customers within that organization and the cloud may exist on or off the customer's premises. In a community cloud, the service is set up for organizations with similar requirements. The cloud may be managed by the organizations or a third party and may exist on or off the organization's premises. A public cloud is available to the general public and is owned and operated by the service provider. A hybrid cloud is a composite of two or more of the above deployment models (private, community, or public) that are bound together by standardized or proprietary technology that enables data and application portability.

[c]FedRAMP is a governmentwide program initiated by the Office of Management and Budget to provide joint authorizations and continuous security monitoring services for cloud computing services. FedRAMP is intended to (1) ensure that cloud computing services have adequate information security; (2) eliminate duplication of effort and reduce

risk management costs; and (3) enable rapid and cost-effective procurement of
information systems/services for federal agencies.

HHS

Cloud computing service	Description of service to be provided	Service model[a]	Deployment model[b]	FedRAMP approved/compliant?[c]
Public Engagement Platform (Software)	Provide the public and federal government with, among other things, mental health and substance abuse prevention and treatment information and associated services through a large-scale information dissemination program.	Software	private	no[d]
Public Engagement Platform (Infrastructure)	Provide the public and the federal government with, among other things, mental health and substance abuse prevention and treatment information and associated services through a large-scale information dissemination program.	Infrastructure	private	yes
National Practitioner Data Bank: Customer Service Center	Enable customer relationship management, call routing, and help desk management software to authorized users including state licensing authorities; medical malpractice payers; hospitals and other health care entities; and licensed health care practitioners.	Software	public	yes
Grantsolutions.gov	Support a comprehensive grants management system for the department, with interactive input and retrieval, allowing users to perform grants management functions.	Infrastructure	public	yes
Public Engagement Platform	Provide the public and the federal government with, among other things, mental health and substance abuse prevention and treatment information and associated services through a large-scale information dissemination program	Infrastructure	private	no[d]
Enterprise Identity Management Multi-Factor Authentication Service	Enable third-party authentication services for the Centers for Medicare & Medicaid Services computer systems by providing registered computer users with access.	Software	public	no
Health Plan Management System	Provide web hosting to support the Medicare Advantage and Prescription Drug Part D programs (which provide optional benefits for prescription drugs to all people with Medicare.)	Infrastructure	private	no[d]

Cloud computing service	Description of service to be provided	Service model[a]	Deployment model[b]	FedRAMP approved/compliant?[c]
Enterprise Identity Management for Medicare and Medicaid	Provide a single electronic credential to an individual to enable access to Centers for Medicare & Medicaid Services systems.	Software	private	no[d]
Collaboration Application Lifecycle Tool	Provide application life-cycle management tools to the Centers for Medicaid & Medicare Services; the tools include project management, documentation management, and software development services.	Platform	private	no[d]
Federally Facilitated Marketplace	Enable Health and Human Services to maintain records used to support Health Insurance Exchange Programs established by the Centers for Medicare & Medicaid Services.	Platform	private	no[d]
Health Resources and Services Administration Emergency Response System	Maintain an emergency response notification system to the department's Health Resources and Services Administration stakeholders.	Software	public	no
Administration for Children and Families Public Web Site	Provide web development services, web-based document management, and portal technology for HHS's Administration for Children and Families.	Infrastructure	public	yes
Remote Identity Proofing	Allow third-party remote identity proofing services for the Centers for Medicare and Medicaid Services stakeholders.	Software	public	no
Web Hosting and Content Management	Enable staff to create and edit documents prior to being posted on the National Institute of Biomedical Imaging and Bioengineering web site.	Platform	public	no
drugabuse.gov public website	Host the National Institute on Drug Abuse public web sites.	Infrastructure	public	yes
Salesforce.com	Provide IT service management software for the National Institutes of Health.	Software	public	yes
National Database for Autism Research	Support HHS's National Institutes of Health-funded research data repository that aims to accelerate progress in autism spectrum disorders research through data sharing, data harmonization, and reporting results.	Infrastructure	public	yes
Alcohol Policy Information System	Support HHS's Alcohol Policy Information System public web sites.	Infrastructure	public	yes
Web Content Management System (Infrastructure)	Provide a system to manage web content and a public web site for the National Institutes of Health	Infrastructure	public	yes

Cloud computing service	Description of service to be provided	Service model[a]	Deployment model[b]	FedRAMP approved/compliant?[c]
Web Content Management System	Provide a system to manage web content and a public web site for the National Institutes of Health	Infrastructure	public	yes
ServiceNow	Support an HHS component agency's IT operations management tool suite. Specifically, the National Institutes of Health uses ServiceNow for incident management, problem management, knowledge management, and service requests.	Software	public	no
Google Analytics	Enable hosted web site analytics.	Software	public	no
FDA.gov	Provide Food and Drug Administration -related information to all interested parties. The web site provides information on (1) product areas that the agency regulates, (2) food and drug advisories, and (3) other agency activities.	Software	public	no
IdeaScale	Support the following features for the Center for Tobacco Products: portal to communicate with the public and other stakeholders; social media platform to provide tobacco product information; tools to conduct qualitative research and export data; and user subscription functionality.	Software	public	no
Virtual Audit Management System	Provide an audit tool to support the Center for Consumer Information and Insurance Oversight, which allows the user to create and manage analysis, audits, and examinations, among other things.	Platform	private	no[d]
State Exchange Resource and Tracking System	Allow HHS to share content, relationship, and case management with state exchange grantees.	Platform	private	no[d]
Data Service Hub	Facilitate the exchange of data between state exchanges, federal exchanges, and federal agencies. Enables verification of coverage eligibility, data payment for issuers, and use of health exchanges for consumers.	Platform	private	no[d]
Customer Services Inquiries	Enable Centers for Medicare & Medicaid Services staff the ability to resolve facilities, telecommunications, and other customer service issues. It also is to include a frequently asked questions function.	Software	public	yes

Cloud computing service	Description of service to be provided	Service model[a]	Deployment model[b]	FedRAMP approved/compliant?[c]
Office of Refugee Resettlement	Provide a general support system for the Office of Refugee Resettlement.	Software	public	no
340B Drug Pricing Program	Maintain a web-based database system to register, track and report participating safety net providers, contracted pharmacy arrangements, and pharmaceutical manufacturers involved in a drug pricing program (called the 340B Drug Pricing Program) administered by the department.	Infrastructure	private	yes
Agency for Healthcare Research and Quality, Quality Indicators Web Site	Provide health care decision-making and research tools to determine health care quality using available hospital inpatient administrative data. The tools are to be used by federal, state, and local officials; researchers; and others that assess health care service quality.	Infrastructure	public	yes
Effective Health Care Web Site	Provide individual researchers, research centers, and academic organizations with an online portal to work together with the Agency for Healthcare Research and Quality to produce research for clinicians, consumers, and policymakers.	Infrastructure	public	yes
Indian Health Service Web Conferencing (Adobe Connect Pro)	Enable agency staff access to collaboration services to be used for meetings and Healthcare training sessions.	Software	public	no
BioSense 2	Enable participants of this service (e.g., the Department of Veteran Affairs, Department of Defense, and civilian hospitals) to control their portion of the cloud and its data used for carrying out each agency's public health surveillance mission. It also is to provide local and state service users free data storage space, a data display dashboard, and a shared environment where users can collaborate on public health surveillance. The BioSense 2.0 cloud computing environment is to be governed jointly by local, state, and federal public health representatives.	Infrastructure	private	yes

Cloud computing service	Description of service to be provided	Service model[a]	Deployment model[b]	FedRAMP approved/compliant?[c]
Centers for Disease Control and Prevention, Mail Exchange	Maintain and update e-mail security software (i.e., anti-SPAM, anti-virus, and malware protection) deployed on the Centers for Disease Control and Prevention IT infrastructure.	Software	private	no[d]
Office 365	Provide applications (Lync, Exchange, SharePoint, etc.) to staff members of the Office of Inspector General.	Software	private	yes

Source: GAO analysis of Department of Health and Human Services data. I GAO-14-753

[a]According to the National Institute of Standards and Technology (NIST), cloud computing offers three models describing the type of IT service to be provided; they include; software as a service, platform as a service, and infrastructure as a service. For infrastructure as a service, the service provider delivers and manages the basic computing infrastructure of servers, software, storage, and network equipment on which a platform (i.e., operating system and programming tools and services) to develop and execute applications can be developed by the consumer. For platform as a service, the service provider delivers and manages the underlying infrastructure, as well as the platform on which the consumer can create applications using programming tools supported by the service provider or other sources. For software as a service, the service provider delivers one or more applications and the computational resources and underlying infrastructure to run them for use on demand as a turnkey service.

[b]NIST has defined four models for how cloud services can be deployed; they are: private, community, public, and hybrid. In a private cloud, the service is set up specifically for one organization, although there may be multiple customers within that organization and the cloud may exist on or off the customer's premises. In a community cloud, the service is set up for organizations with similar requirements. The cloud may be managed by the organizations or a third party and may exist on or off the organization's premises. A public cloud is available to the general public and is owned and operated by the service provider. A hybrid cloud is a composite of two or more of the above deployment models (private, community, or public) that are bound together by standardized or proprietary technology that enables data and application portability.

[c]FedRAMP is a governmentwide program initiated by the Office of Management and Budget to provide joint authorizations and continuous security monitoring services for cloud computing services. FedRAMP is intended to (1) ensure that cloud computing services have adequate information security; (2) eliminate duplication of effort and reduce risk management costs; and (3) enable rapid and cost-effective procurement of information systems/services for federal agencies.

[d]Although HHS reported this service as being neither FedRAMP approved nor compliant, the department also reported that the service did not need to be so because FedRAMP does not require these types of services (i.e., private cloud services) to be compliant with its requirements.

SBA

Cloud computing service	Description of service to be provided	Service model[a]	Deployment model[b]	FedRAMP approved/compliant?[c]
Human Resources (InCompass)	Implement a performance management module for the agency that captures employees' performance goals and tracks accomplishments throughout the fiscal year.	Software	private	no
Local Area Network/Wide Area Network (LiveVault)	Provide online backup and recovery capabilities; and electronic vaulting for records retention for the department.	Infrastructure	public	no
Capital Planning and Investment Control and IT Governance	Support services that enable the agency to complete its capital planning and investment control reporting.	Software	private	no
IT Investments for Enterprise Architecture, IT Quality Assurance	Provide a business intelligence tool to assist agency staff in managing organizational artifacts through an enterprise data repository.	Software	private	yes

Source: GAO analysis of Small Business Administration data. I GAO-14-753

[a]According to the National Institute of Standards and Technology (NIST), cloud computing offers three models describing the type of IT service to be provided; they include; software as a service, platform as a service, and infrastructure as a service. For infrastructure as a service, the service provider delivers and manages the basic computing infrastructure of servers, software, storage, and network equipment on which a platform (i.e., operating system and programming tools and services) to develop and execute applications can be developed by the consumer. For platform as a service, the service provider delivers and manages the underlying infrastructure, as well as the platform on which the consumer can create applications using programming tools supported by the service provider or other sources. For software as a service, the service provider delivers one or more applications and the computational resources and underlying infrastructure to run them for use on demand as a turnkey service.

[b]NIST has defined four models for how cloud services can be deployed; they are: private, community, public, and hybrid. In a private cloud, the service is set up specifically for one organization, although there may be multiple customers within that organization and the cloud may exist on or off the customer's premises. In a community cloud, the service is set up for organizations with similar requirements. The cloud may be managed by the organizations or a third party and may exist on or off the organization's premises. A public cloud is available to the general public and is owned and operated by the service provider. A hybrid cloud is a composite of two or more of the above deployment models (private, community, or public) that are bound together by standardized or proprietary technology that enables data and application portability.

[c]FedRAMP is a governmentwide program initiated by the Office of Management and Budget to provide joint authorizations and continuous security monitoring services for cloud computing services. FedRAMP is intended to (1) ensure that cloud computing services have adequate information security; (2) eliminate duplication of effort and reduce risk management costs; and (3) enable rapid and cost-effective procurement of information systems/services for federal agencies.

State

Cloud computing service	Description of service to be provided	Service model[a]	Deployment model[b]	FedRAMP approved/compliant?[c]
Foreign Assistance Coordination and Tracking System	Provide a tool to be used for budget planning and formulation, and performance reporting. The tool also is to provide the means to generate reports to respond to ad hoc queries from Congress and other stakeholders about the use of foreign assistance resources.	Infrastructure	public	yes
Non Proliferation and Disarmament Fund	Allow program managers of the Nonproliferation and Disarmament Fund access to agency data from any staff work location.	Platform	public	yes
Ralph Bunche Electronic Library	Provide domestic and overseas agency staff with direct access to information in over 50 databases. The service is also to provide additional functionality including an integrated electronic catalog with other online libraries.	Software	public	no
Content Management System	Support a collaboration and knowledge management environment for the department which includes hosting for servers and applications, and an environment for application development and product testing.	Infrastructure	public/ private	yes
State Assistance Management System	Provide a grants management system for the department which supports the full life cycle of the federal assistance process.	Software	private	yes
State Department Web Site	Enable the hosting of public web sites for the Department of State, including its embassies.	Platform	public	yes
Travel Manager Program	Provide a web-based travel management service for the department.	Software	private/ community	yes
Office of Historian	Enable unclassified documents to be available worldwide regarding the history of the department, diplomacy, and foreign relations.	Infrastructure	public	yes
Application Services	Provide application services for the department, including application integration.	Infrastructure	private	no
Electronic Forms	Support the department's centralized electronic forms program.	Platform	private	no
Joint Financial Management System	Provide support for a key departmental financial management system's (the Joint Financial Management System) continuity of operations component.	Infrastructure	private	no

Cloud computing service	Description of service to be provided	Service model[a]	Deployment model[b]	FedRAMP approved/compliant?[c]
Continuity of Operations Planning	Support the Executive Secretariat's continuity of operations planning.	Infrastructure	private	no
Worldwide Remote Email System	Provide departmental personnel with the capability to remotely access e-mail worldwide.	Infrastructure	private	no
Security/Cyber Security Services	Provide the department's Bureau of Diplomatic Security with an enterprise service operations center.	Infrastructure	private	no

Source: GAO analysis of Department of State data. I GAO-14-753

[a]According to the National Institute of Standards and Technology (NIST), cloud computing offers three models describing the type of IT service to be provided; they include; software as a service, platform as a service, and infrastructure as a service. For infrastructure as a service, the service provider delivers and manages the basic computing infrastructure of servers, software, storage, and network equipment on which a platform (i.e., operating system and programming tools and services) to develop and execute applications can be developed by the consumer. For platform as a service, the service provider delivers and manages the underlying infrastructure, as well as the platform on which the consumer can create applications using programming tools supported by the service provider or other sources. For software as a service, the service provider delivers one or more applications and the computational resources and underlying infrastructure to run them for use on demand as a turnkey service.

[b]NIST has defined four models for how cloud services can be deployed; they are: private, community, public, and hybrid. In a private cloud, the service is set up specifically for one organization, although there may be multiple customers within that organization and the cloud may exist on or off the customer's premises. In a community cloud, the service is set up for organizations with similar requirements. The cloud may be managed by the organizations or a third party and may exist on or off the organization's premises. A public cloud is available to the general public and is owned and operated by the service provider. A hybrid cloud is a composite of two or more of the above deployment models (private, community, or public) that are bound together by standardized or proprietary technology that enables data and application portability.

[c]FedRAMP is a governmentwide program initiated by the Office of Management and Budget to provide joint authorizations and continuous security monitoring services for cloud computing services. FedRAMP is intended to (1) ensure that cloud computing services have adequate information security; (2) eliminate duplication of effort and reduce risk management costs; and (3) enable rapid and cost-effective procurement of information systems/services for federal agencies.

Treasury

Cloud computing service	Description of service to be provided	Service model[a]	Deployment model[b]	FedRAMP approved/compliant?[c]
Franchise Financial and Administrative Services	Provide financial management services to the department via a web-enabled, integrated, accounting, budgeting, procurement, and reporting commercial off-the-shelf system.	Software	hybrid	no
IRS.GOV - Portal Environment	Enable web-based services to internal and external users, such as taxpayers, Internal Revenue Service employees, and other government agencies, as part of administering the federal tax code.	Infrastructure	public	no
Manufacturing Support Suite	Support an integrated system for managing the Bureau of Engraving and Printing's day-to-day business and manufacturing operations.	Platform	private	yes
Treasury Web Solutions	Support the department's internal and external web sites. If offers a full suite of web solutions including hosting, design, development, and deployment to web sites.	Platform, Software	community	yes
Enterprise Asset Management System	Enable the Bureau of Engraving and Printing to manage bureau assets during their entire life cycle, from acquisition through decommissioning.	Platform	private	yes

Source: GAO analysis of Department of Treasury data. I GAO-14-753

[a]According to the National Institute of Standards and Technology (NIST), cloud computing offers three models describing the type of IT service to be provided; they include; software as a service, platform as a service, and infrastructure as a service. For infrastructure as a service, the service provider delivers and manages the basic computing infrastructure of servers, software, storage, and network equipment on which a platform (i.e., operating system and programming tools and services) to develop and execute applications can be developed by the consumer. For platform as a service, the service provider delivers and manages the underlying infrastructure, as well as the platform on which the consumer can create applications using programming tools supported by the service provider or other sources. For software as a service, the service provider delivers one or more applications and the computational resources and underlying infrastructure to run them for use on demand as a turnkey service.

[b]NIST has defined four models for how cloud services can be deployed; they are: private, community, public, and hybrid. In a private cloud, the service is set up specifically for one organization, although there may be multiple customers within that organization and the cloud may exist on or off the customer's premises. In a community cloud, the service is set up for organizations with similar requirements. The cloud may be managed by the organizations or a third party and may exist on or off the organization's premises. A public cloud is available to the general public and is owned and operated by the service provider. A hybrid cloud is a composite of two or more of the above deployment models (private, community, or public) that are bound together by standardized or proprietary technology that enables data and application portability.

[c]FedRAMP is a governmentwide program initiated by the Office of Management and Budget to provide joint authorizations and continuous security monitoring services for cloud computing services. FedRAMP is intended to (1) ensure that cloud computing services have adequate information security; (2) eliminate duplication of effort and reduce

risk management costs; and (3) enable rapid and cost-effective procurement of
information systems/services for federal agencies.

USDA

Cloud computing service	Description of service to be provided	Service model[a]	Deployment model[b]	FedRAMP approved/compliant?[c]
ArcGIS Online (public)	Provide a cloud-based geospatial service that supports data and the geographic information system. It creates web map/feature services, asset exchange, versioning, templates, and cost controls for external publication of products and services.	Infrastructure, Platform and Software	public	no
ArcGIS Online (private)	Provide an internal cloud-based geospatial shared service that supports data and the geographic information system. It improves cost controls by modernizing and/or creating functions of discovery and reuse, uniform web map/feature services, asset exchange, versioning, templates, group workflows and collaboration, and enables an integrated development environment.	Platform and Software	private	no
Electronic Capital Planning and Investment Control	Maintain a government-owned, web-based application that is designed to help agencies in the management and control of their initiatives, portfolios, and investment priorities, as well as in the preparation and submission of budget data to OMB.	Software	private	no
e-Training	Support an electronic training system for the department that provides online administration of curriculum by trainers, individualized training support, on-demand classroom registration, customized content, collaborative tools, and integrated back-end systems.	Software	public/private	no
Freedom of Information Act Xpress	Allow the department to track, process, and redact materials requested under the Freedom of Information Act.	Software	public	yes
Microsoft Office 365	Provide IT communication services used by USDA organizations. It is to provide integrated communications tools for USDA's approximately 120,000 employees and business partners.	Software	public	no
National IT Center Infrastructure as a Service Server	Provide customers with platform services to support the development and transition of business applications into standardized enterprise data center service offerings.	Infrastructure	private	yes

Cloud computing service	Description of service to be provided	Service model[a]	Deployment model[b]	FedRAMP approved/compliant?[c]
National IT Center Platform as a Service Server	Provide operating platforms to securely host customer applications. As part of this, the National IT Center is to utilize advanced server virtualization technologies, strict standards, and economies of scale to enable rapid delivery of cost-effective, fully-managed operating platforms with expanded inheritable security controls.	Platform	private	yes
Salesforce 1 Platform	Support a single system for tracking and managing correspondence across USDA, including Secretarial and agency correspondence. It is to include modern Customer Relationship Management features and mobile device access.	Platform	public	no
Web Accelerator	Provide delivery benefits for all content types. It also is to provide increased availability and other performance benefits as well as a scalable on-demand network.	Platform	public	yes

Source: GAO analysis of Department of Agriculture data. I GAO-14-753

[a]According to the National Institute of Standards and Technology (NIST), cloud computing offers three models describing the type of IT service to be provided; they include; software as a service, platform as a service, and infrastructure as a service. For infrastructure as a service, the service provider delivers and manages the basic computing infrastructure of servers, software, storage, and network equipment on which a platform (i.e., operating system and programming tools and services) to develop and execute applications can be developed by the consumer. For platform as a service, the service provider delivers and manages the underlying infrastructure, as well as the platform on which the consumer can create applications using programming tools supported by the service provider or other sources. For software as a service, the service provider delivers one or more applications and the computational resources and underlying infrastructure to run them for use on demand as a turnkey service.

[b]NIST has defined four models for how cloud services can be deployed; they are: private, community, public, and hybrid. In a private cloud, the service is set up specifically for one organization, although there may be multiple customers within that organization and the cloud may exist on or off the customer's premises. In a community cloud, the service is set up for organizations with similar requirements. The cloud may be managed by the organizations or a third party and may exist on or off the organization's premises. A public cloud is available to the general public and is owned and operated by the service provider. A hybrid cloud is a composite of two or more of the above deployment models (private, community, or public) that are bound together by standardized or proprietary technology that enables data and application portability.

[c]FedRAMP is a governmentwide program initiated by the Office of Management and Budget to provide joint authorizations and continuous security monitoring services for cloud computing services. FedRAMP is intended to (1) ensure that cloud computing services have adequate information security; (2) eliminate duplication of effort and reduce risk management costs; and (3) enable rapid and cost-effective procurement of information systems/services for federal agencies.

Appendix III: Comments from the Department of Homeland Security

Homeland
Security

September 16, 2014

David A. Powner
Director, Information Technology Management Issues
U.S. Government Accountability Office
441 G Street, NW
Washington, DC 20548

Re: Draft Report GAO-14-753, "CLOUD COMPUTING: Additional Opportunities and
Savings Need to Be Pursued"

Dear Mr. Powner:

Thank you for the opportunity to review and comment on this draft report. The U.S. Department
of Homeland Security (DHS) appreciates the U.S. Government Accountability Office's (GAO)
work in planning and conducting its review and issuing this report.

The Department is pleased to note GAO's positive recognition that DHS has saved
$34.10 million by implementing cloud computing services. GAO also highlighted that DHS has
implemented five additional cloud computing services since GAO's last review in July 2012.
DHS is committed to successfully maturing and optimizing the Department's cloud computing
capabilities to address many of the daily challenges the Department faces, such as reducing
Information Technology (IT) operating and unit costs, delivering high value to stakeholders,
meeting the demand for new technologies to support mission, mitigating financial risks, and
delivering reliable and secure solutions across the Department.

The draft report contains two recommendations with which the Department concurs.
Specifically, GAO recommended that the Secretary of Homeland Security:

Recommendation 1: Ensure that all IT investments are assessed for suitability for migration to
a cloud computing service.

Response: Concur. The DHS Office of the Chief Information Officer (OCIO) will use the
existing Enterprise Business Management Office's IT Portfolio annual review process and DHS
systems inventory to assess the suitability of DHS investments for migrating to a cloud
environment. Additionally, OCIO will work with Components to identify potential cloud
migration pilot projects. Estimated Completion Date (ECD): December 31, 2014.

Recommendation 2: Establish evaluation dates for those investments identified in this report
that have not been assessed for migration to the cloud.

Response: Concur. The DHS OCIO will establish evaluation dates for those systems that fall under the investments identified in the report that have not been assessed for migration to the cloud. ECD: To be provided within 60 calendar days after formal transmittal of GAO's final report to the Department.

Again, thank you for the opportunity to review and comment on this draft report. Technical comments were provided under separate cover. Please feel free to contact me if you have any questions. We look forward to working with you in the future.

Sincerely,

Jim H. Crumpacker, CIA, CFE
Director
Departmental GAO-OIG Liaison Office

2

Appendix IV: Comments from the General Services Administration

The Administrator

September 10, 2014

The Honorable Gene L. Dodaro
Comptroller General of the United States
U.S. Government Accountability Office
Washington, DC 20548

Dear Mr. Dodaro:

The U.S. General Services Administration (GSA) appreciates the opportunity to review and comment on the draft report, *Cloud Computing: Additional Opportunities and Savings Need to Be Pursued*, (GAO-14-753). The U.S. Government Accountability Office (GAO) recommends that the GSA Administrator:

- Ensure that all IT investments are assessed for suitability for migration to a cloud computing service.

- As part of this, establish evaluation dates for those services identified in this report that have not been assessed for migration to the cloud.

We agree with the findings and recommendations and will take appropriate action. If you have any questions or concerns, please contact me at (202) 501-0800, or Ms. Lisa Austin, Associate Administrator, Office of Congressional and Intergovernmental Affairs, at (202) 501-0563.

Sincerely,

Dan Tangherlini
Administrator

cc: David A. Powner, Director, Information Technology Management Issues, GAO

1800 F Street, NW
Washington, DC 20405-0002

www.gsa.gov

Appendix V: Comments from the Department of State

United States Department of State

Comptroller

P.O. Box 150008
Charleston, SC 29415-5008

SEP 1 2 2014

Dr. Loren Yager
Managing Director
International Affairs and Trade
Government Accountability Office
441 G Street, N.W.
Washington, D.C. 20548-0001

Dear Dr. Yager:

We appreciate the opportunity to review your draft report, "CLOUD COMPUTING: Additional Opportunities and Savings Need to Be Pursued" GAO Job Code 311296.

The enclosed Department of State comments are provided for incorporation with this letter as an appendix to the final report.

If you have any questions concerning this response, please contact Minh-Hai Tran-Lam, Director, Bureau of Information Resource Management, Office of Strategic Planning at (202) 634-3647.

Sincerely,

Christopher H. Flaggs, Acting

Enclosure:
As stated.

cc: GAO – David Powner
       IRM – Steven Taylor
       State/OIG – Norman Brown

Department of State Response to GAO Draft Report
CLOUD COMPUTING: Additional Opportunities and
Savings Need to Be Pursued
(GAO-14-753; GAO Code 311296)

The Department of State welcomes the opportunity to respond to the GAO
draft report, *"Cloud Computing: Additional Opportunities and Savings Need to Be
Pursued."*

To help ensure continued progress in the implementation of cloud
computing services, GAO recommended that the Secretaries of Agriculture, Health
and Human Services, Homeland Security, State and the Treasury; and the
Administrators of the General Services Administration and Small Business
Administration direct their respective Chief Information Officers to take the
following actions:

- Ensure that all Information Technology (IT) investments are assessed for
  suitability for migration to a cloud computing service.
- As part of this, establish evaluation dates for those services identified in
  this report that have not been assessed for mitigation to the cloud.

The Department of State has already addressed these recommendations. The
Department of State has already developed and communicated guidance to IT
investment owners on how to implement OMB guidance in the Cloud First policy.

All IT investments, major and non-majors, are currently performing cloud
computing analysis of alternatives. State expects to complete all analyses by the
end of the current calendar year, CY2014.

Appendix VI: Comments from the Department of the Treasury

DEPARTMENT OF THE TREASURY
WASHINGTON, D.C.

SEP 9 2014

Mr. David A. Powner
Director
Information Technology Management Issues
U.S. Government Accountability Office
441 G Street, NW
Washington, DC 20548

Dear Mr. Powner,

Thank you for the opportunity to provide comments on GAO's Draft Report, *"Cloud Computing: Additional Opportunities and Savings Need to Be Pursued (GAO-14-753)."* The Department of the Treasury has no comments on the Report and appreciates GAO's efforts in its development.

Please contact me at 202-622-1200 if you need anything further.

Sincerely,

Raghav Vajjhala
Acting Deputy Assistant Secretary for Information
Systems and Chief Information Officer

Appendix VII: GAO Contact and Staff Acknowledgments

GAO Contact	David A. Powner, (202) 512-9286 or pownerd@gao.gov
Staff Acknowledgments	In addition to the contact name above, individuals making contributions to this report included Gary Mountjoy (assistant director), Gerard Aflague, Scott Borre, Nancy Glover, and Lori Martinez.

GAO's Mission	The Government Accountability Office, the audit, evaluation, and investigative arm of Congress, exists to support Congress in meeting its constitutional responsibilities and to help improve the performance and accountability of the federal government for the American people. GAO examines the use of public funds; evaluates federal programs and policies; and provides analyses, recommendations, and other assistance to help Congress make informed oversight, policy, and funding decisions. GAO's commitment to good government is reflected in its core values of accountability, integrity, and reliability.
Obtaining Copies of GAO Reports and Testimony	The fastest and easiest way to obtain copies of GAO documents at no cost is through GAO's website (www.gao.gov). Each weekday afternoon, GAO posts on its website newly released reports, testimony, and correspondence. To have GAO e-mail you a list of newly posted products, go to www.gao.gov and select "E-mail Updates."
Order by Phone	The price of each GAO publication reflects GAO's actual cost of production and distribution and depends on the number of pages in the publication and whether the publication is printed in color or black and white. Pricing and ordering information is posted on GAO's website, http://www.gao.gov/ordering.htm. Place orders by calling (202) 512-6000, toll free (866) 801-7077, or TDD (202) 512-2537. Orders may be paid for using American Express, Discover Card, MasterCard, Visa, check, or money order. Call for additional information.
Connect with GAO	Connect with GAO on Facebook, Flickr, Twitter, and YouTube. Subscribe to our RSS Feeds or E-mail Updates. Listen to our Podcasts. Visit GAO on the web at www.gao.gov.
To Report Fraud, Waste, and Abuse in Federal Programs	Contact: Website: www.gao.gov/fraudnet/fraudnet.htm E-mail: fraudnet@gao.gov Automated answering system: (800) 424-5454 or (202) 512-7470
Congressional Relations	Katherine Siggerud, Managing Director, siggerudk@gao.gov, (202) 512-4400, U.S. Government Accountability Office, 441 G Street NW, Room 7125, Washington, DC 20548
Public Affairs	Chuck Young, Managing Director, youngc1@gao.gov, (202) 512-4800 U.S. Government Accountability Office, 441 G Street NW, Room 7149 Washington, DC 20548

www.ingramcontent.com/pod-product-compliance
Lightning Source LLC
Chambersburg PA
CBHW060506060326
40689CB00020B/4655